# THE FIRST RIDE

## BLAZING THE TRAIL FOR THE PONY EXPRESS

### BY JACQUELINE GEIS

IDEALS CHILDREN'S BOOKS • NASHVILLE, TENNESSEE

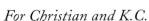

Published by Ideals Children's Books
An imprint of Hambleton-Hill Publishing, Inc.
Nashville, Tennessee 37218

Printed and bound in Mexico

**Library of Congress Cataloging-in-Publication Data**
Geis, Jacqueline, 1955–
    The first ride : blazing the trail for the Pony Express / written and illustrated by Jacqueline Geis.
        p.    cm.
    ISBN 1-57102-004-7
    1. Pony express—History—Juvenile literature. 2. Postal service—United States—History—Juvenile literature. 3. Express service—United States—History—Juvenile literature. [1. Pony express.] I. Title.
    HE6375.P65G44        1994
    363'.143'0973—dc20                                          94-7009
                                                                CIP
                                                                AC

The illustrations in this book were rendered in watercolors.
The text type is set in Caslon Regular.
The display type is set in Caslon Antique.
Color separations were made by Web Tech, Inc.
Printed and bound by R.R. Donnelley & Sons.

First Edition
10 9 8 7 6 5 4 3 2 1

*For Christian and K.C.*

*Special thanks to B.G., M.G., A.B., J.F., C.C., S.H., R.J., and Yolie.*

—J.G.

The publisher wishes to thank Jacqueline Lewin, historian of the Pony Express National Memorial in St. Joseph, Missouri, for reviewing and verifying the historical accuracy of The First Ride.

# WANTED
## YOUNG SKINNY WIRY FELLOWS

not over eighteen. Must be expert

riders willing to risk death daily.

Orphans preferred. WAGES $25 per

week. Apply, *Central Overland*

*Express, Alta Bldg., Montgomery St.*

IN 1860, I WAS HIRED BY THE CENTRAL OVERLAND CALIFORNIA AND PIKE'S Peak Express Company to ride for the Pony Express. I was given a small Bible and was asked to sign a pledge. All riders had to promise never to use bad language, drink alcohol, or fight with other riders. We also had to promise to be honest and faithful in our jobs and to use our weapons only in self-defense.

Riders traveled both ways—east and west—on the Pony Express trail. The ride west started in St. Joseph, Missouri, while the ride east began in Sacramento, California. I was the first eastbound rider, picking up mail in Sacramento and carrying it to my home station at Sportsman's Hall. There I would wait for a little over nine days for the westbound mail to reach me. Then it would be back to Sacramento, carrying news of the east to that city.

Our orders were to stay on schedule, no matter what happened.

Our motto was: "The mail must go through."

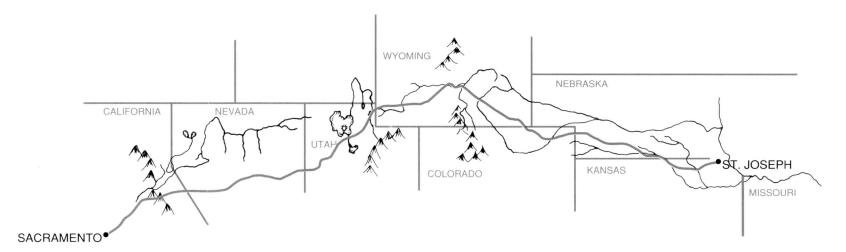

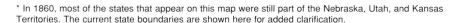

* In 1860, most of the states that appear on this map were still part of the Nebraska, Utah, and Kansas Territories. The current state boundaries are shown here for added clarification.

As the sun was peeking through the snow clouds, my first eastbound ride was coming to an end. I could see my home station up ahead in the town of Sportsman's Hall. It was a welcome sight, for I had just ridden sixty miles east from Sacramento, and I was tired and cold.

The stationkeeper grabbed my sturdy, snorting mustang as I arrived. He gave my leather mail pouch—called a *mochila* (moe-CHEE-la)—to the waiting rider and sent him on his way toward the east.

"What's your name, son?" asked the stationkeeper.

"Billy Hamilton," I replied through my chattering teeth. Wiping my red, runny nose on my sleeve, I went inside the cabin to warm myself. As I stood in front of the fire, the feeling in my numb-to-the-bones fingers returned. My stomach began to howl like a coyote as the smell of bacon and beans in a pot hanging over the flames tickled and tempted my nose.

After I had hung my cold, wet clothes by the fire, the stationkeeper came in. He stomped the snow from his boots and rustled up a plate of beans and cornbread and a tin cup of coffee for me. For the next nine days we would share chores, dreams, and tall tales of the trail, waiting while other Pony Express riders carried the westbound mail toward my station.

Just fifteen hours before I arrived at Sportsman's Hall, a celebration had begun in the town of St. Joseph, Missouri. Flags of all kinds and colors rippled and waved from the town buildings while a brass band played. Men, women, and children, dressed in their best, had come to see the westbound Pony Express take off for the two-thousand-mile trip to Sacramento, California.

The thought that mail could reach the west coast in only ten days was almost impossible to believe. In the excitement, the crowd spooked the horse chosen for the first run. Some even tried to pull hairs from her tail to keep as souvenirs.

The people in the crowd became restless when they were told that the train carrying the mail from Washington, D.C., was more than two hours late. At last they heard the whistle of the train and the sound of the engine rushing and roaring at the edge of town.

A cannon fired a smoky salute after the mayor and company officials shouted their speeches. Johnny Fry was dressed in a red shirt, blue jeans, boots, and slouch hat, and carried a shiny revolver in a "Slim Jim" holster. He put the mochila on his saddle and mounted his horse. He rode a few blocks to the west, to the ferryboat that would float him across the Missouri River to Elwood in Kansas Territory.

After the ferry docked, Fry continued on his way, racing toward the west. He had started two-and-a-half hours behind schedule, so he rode hard from relay station to station in order to make up the lost time.

Don Rising, who was barely old enough to grow a beard, took the mochila from Johnny Fry at Seneca and carried it to Marysville. The leather mochila was used to carry the mail because it fit over the saddle and was easily passed from one rider to the next. Attached to the mochila were four boxes called *cantinas* (kan-TEE-nuz). Three cantinas were locked and one was kept open to receive the mail. The locked cantinas could only be opened with keys guarded in the post offices at St. Joseph and Sacramento.

Rising arrived in Marysville just about the time I was settling in at Sportsman's Hall.

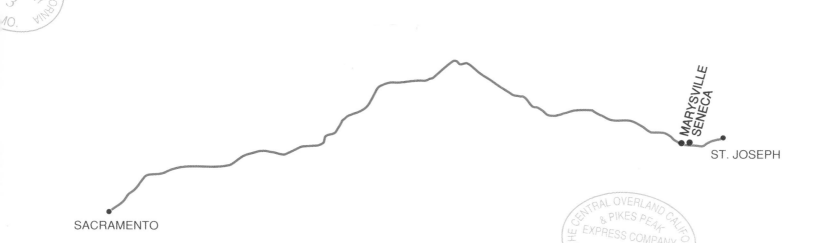

SACRAMENTO

MARYSVILLE
SENECA

ST. JOSEPH

Jack Keetley, waiting at the Marysville station, grabbed the mochila from Rising and carried it through stations called Hollenburg, Rock Creek, and Big Sandy.

Henry Wallace, on his Kentucky-bred horse, rode through the prairie grass so fast he could set it on fire. He took the mochila through Liberty Farm and on to Fort Kearny.

Immigrants who were riding in a stagecoach on the Oregon Trail strained their necks, like turtles in their shells, to get a glimpse of a Pony Express rider passing by. The rider was Barney Wintle, headed for

Cottonwood Springs, hunched down in the saddle behind his horse's mane. Riding as if he had seen the ghost of an Indian spirit, he dodged and darted around the stagecoach.

Some think the eastbound and westbound riders passed each other somewhere east of Salt Lake City. An eagle in the sky was probably the only witness to this event.

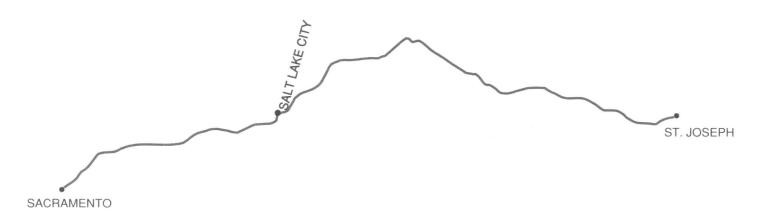

SALT LAKE CITY

ST. JOSEPH

SACRAMENTO

Richard Egan galloped across the wide desert floor, blinking his eyes at the mirages he saw on his seventy-five-mile trip to Rush Valley.

William Dennis took over next, blazing a trail to Egan Canyon.

William Fisher rode through mountain ranges where every rock, tree, and trail looked the same as ten others, making it easy to get lost. A skillful explorer, Fisher found his home station at Ruby Valley.

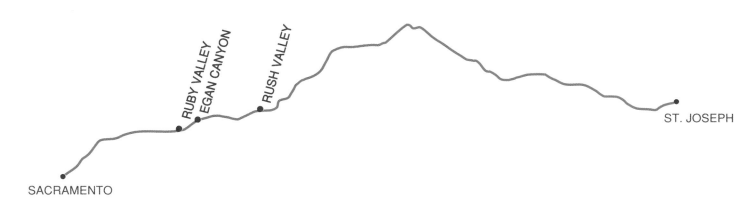

With every change in the wind, "Pony Bob" Haslam breathed in scents of sagebrush and juniper on his route from Buckland's Station, past Carson City, and west to Friday's Station.

While I waited, Warren Upson was riding through the Sierra Nevada Mountains toward my home station. His horse picked his way carefully through the dangerous, narrow trail between the granite cliffs. Upson, in

awe of the towering heights, looked toward the sky at clouds that appeared to beckon to him and guide him safely through the stony passages to Sportsman's Hall.

I heard the rumbling of hoofbeats in the distance and turned in time to see Upson's hat fly off his head. My wait was over. Upson threw me the mochila, and I was on my way.

I was off on my ride back to Sacramento. Remembering my company pledge, I couldn't have been stopped by a blizzard, an earthquake, or a shower of arrows.

SPORTSMAN'S HALL

ST. JOSEPH

SACRAMENTO

Judging the time by watching the sun sink lower in the sky, I knew I was getting close to Sacramento. By dusk, I had reached the edge of town, riding behind a cloud of dust from lookout messengers who rode ahead of me. A bonfire in the street lit the cheering faces of the townspeople. At last their isolation from the rest of the country was ended.

## *Historical Note*

The freighting firm Russell, Majors, and Waddell was the parent company of the Central Overland California and Pike's Peak Express Company, which ran the Pony Express. The company's owners had dreamed up the Pony Express as a way to reduce the time it took messages to reach California. They hoped to be given the great overland mail delivery contract by the U.S. government. They were not awarded this contract.

Only eighteen months after the historic first ride, the company that ran the Pony Express was bankrupt. The arrival of telegraph lines in California meant that mail delivery by horse was no longer needed. But the Pony Express riders had proved that mail could be carried year-round along a northern route. They also showed that this route would be a good line for the telegraph and the railroad. Many people believed that the Pony Express helped to keep California in the Union during the Civil War by quickly delivering important messages along a northern route, where they could not be captured by southern spies.

Today, the Pony Express lives on in the tales of the American Old West. The stables in St. Joseph, Missouri, starting point of that first ride, have been restored. They now house the Pony Express National Memorial, a museum dedicated to preserving the legend of the Pony Express.